The Skinny on Success

the skinny on™

success

why not you?

Jim Randel

ISBN: 978-0-9818935-9-4
Ebook ISBN: 978-0-9841393-4-7
Library of Congress: 2009905897

Illustration/Design: Lindy Nass

For information address Rand Media Co, 265 Post Road West, Westport, CT, 06880 or call (203) 226-8727.

The Skinny On™ books are available for special promotions and premiums. For details contact: Donna Hardy, call (203) 222-6295 or visit our website: www.theskinnyon.com

Printed in the United States of America
10 9 8 7 6 5 4 3
9 2 5 – 4 9 1 9

the skinny on™

Welcome to a new series of publications entitled **The Skinny On™,** a progression of drawings, dialogue and text intended to convey information in a concise and entertaining fashion.

In our time-starved and information-overloaded culture, most of us have far too little time to read. As a result, our understanding of important subjects often tends to float on the surface – without the insights of writings from thinkers and teachers who have spent years studying these subjects.

Our series is intended to address this situation. Our team of readers and researchers has done a ton of homework preparing our books for you. We read everything we could find on the topic at hand and spoke with the experts. Then we mixed in our own experiences and distilled what we have learned into this "skinny" book for your benefit.

Our goal is to do the reading for you, identify what is important, distill the key points, and present them in a book that is both instructive and enjoyable to read.

Although minimalist in design, we do take our message very seriously. Please do not confuse format with content. The time you invest reading this book will be paid back to you many, many times over.

FOREWORD

Webster's Dictionary defines "success" as "the attainment of wealth, favor or eminence."

Success is, of course, different for each of us but for most of us, the obtaining of money, fame or power is right up there. Our book is about these kinds of tangible success. We take no position on the importance of material versus spiritual success (or even whether they are mutually exclusive).

We believe that 99% of the world's success goes to those people who find the courage to pursue their dreams with everything they have. We do not believe that success is somehow reserved for the smartest, most talented, best-looking or even the luckiest. We believe that the likelihood of your achieving your goals and aspirations is a direct function of the heart and will you bring to the pursuit.

Our objective with this book is to help you reflect upon your potential. We are not going to patronize you with the bromide "you can be anything you want to be." The truth is that there are some limitations and factors beyond your control. Still, what every one of us can do is maximize the likelihood of our success. In other words, we can take steps to improve our chances. Throughout this book, we will be highlighting those steps we believe will increase the probability of your attaining that which you seek.

We believe that each of us has enormous upside potential. Our observation is that most people aim too low – not too high. It appears to us that far too many people underestimate their potential and the heights to which they can climb. We hope that this book will find its way into the hands of such people, and that it will inspire them to reach a bit higher.

A WORD FROM THE PUBLISHER

Some of you may ask why we are publishing a book about an important subject like success in a stick-person, story format.

Well, part of it is entertainment value. We want as many people as possible – of all ages, educations and cultures – to engage with our comments. And the truth is that today fewer and fewer people are reading 200-page, single-spaced, small-font volumes.

Another part of it is that there is so much written on the subjects of success and achievement that many people are overwhelmed. We have synthesized what is written so that in the hour or two it takes you to read this book, you will get a great sense of all that is out there.

Finally, we want to strip away all surplus which encumbers the "how to succeed" books. We have studied thousands of successful people and there is a consistent pattern:

99% of success stories are about a person who:

1) Identified an endeavor he or she felt strongly about,

2) Took action in the pursuit thereof, and

3) Persisted against inevitable setbacks.

Those three steps describe the process. While the exact route is different for everyone, success almost always comes down to passion, action and persistence.

We hope that by bringing you information in an easy-to-digest presentation, we will push you to reflect on your own goals and dreams, where you are in the passage to their achievement, and finally what steps you can take to move you closer toward your aspirations.

"Know then, that the world exists for you. For you are the phenomenon perfect. What we are, that only we can see. All that Adam had, all that Caesar could, you have and can do … build therefore your own world."

Ralph Waldo Emerson, *Nature*

Hi, I'm Jim Randel.

Meet Billy and Beth. They met in college. They graduated three years ago. They are seriously dating.

Billy could not find a job when he graduated so he started working for his father's accounting firm. He is studying to become a CPA. It's not what he envisioned for himself.

Beth has always been interested in public service. She works for a law firm as a paralegal. She would like to go into politics some day.

9

10

11

12

13

14

Billy is at an important crossroads. After college he opted for the path of least resistance. He does not really want to be a CPA.

He knows that he needs to make a change.

15

Billy knows that he will never achieve the success he wants unless he finds a pursuit he feels really strongly about ... something he is passionate about.

16

Billy needs to be as precise as possible in identifying his passion … an activity he loves doing.

You see not everyone will realize all of their dreams. But in the pursuit of something you love doing, you can't lose. You have created a lifetime of doing what makes you happy.

17

The clearer you are about what you love doing and what you want to accomplish in life the better. Clarity leads to visualization which fosters achievement.

18

Billy went to the library to find books about the identification of one's passion.

Here are three of the books he found the most helpful:

Flow: The Psychology of Optimal Experience, by Mihaly Csikszentmihalyi

Finding Your North Star: Claiming the Life You Were Meant to Live, by Martha Beck

The Element: How Finding Your Passion Changes Everything, by Ken Robinson

Here are Billy's "take aways" from these books:

1. Identifying your passion is in part a matter of watching for signs.

What are you doing when:

a) you lose track of time during the day?

b) you don't hear barking dogs or loud sirens?

c) you feel centered … relaxed even though engaged in a difficult challenge?

d) you feel energized?

e) you forget to eat?

f) you have a sense of wellness?

g) you can focus easily for long periods of time?

As Marcus Buckingham writes in his best-selling book *Now Discover Your Strengths*:

"Step back and watch yourself."

2. Finding your passion is the first step. Next is creating a living around what you love doing.

Most of us need to make money. Some of us want to make a lot of money. Meshing your passion with your need and desire for money is not always easy of course.

Often choices have to be made. If you love teaching, for example, you will probably never own a Lear Jet.

However, if you pursue what you love doing with all you've got, with every ounce of energy in your body, the money is likely to follow. Perhaps not the Lear Jet but hopefully enough to make a good living … and then some.

"Those who pursue work for just the love of money are most likely not going to find money ... nor work they love."

Anonymous

3. Transitioning from a job or activity that is not right for you into one that is will likely mean incremental steps.

Billy can't just quit his job as he needs to support himself. Most of us are in Billy's situation.

What we can do, however, is take steps to put ourselves in an environment where people are doing what we would like to. Join associations and clubs with like-minded people. Offer to work for free in a situation where your "internship" might transition to employment. Cut back on your sleep to write that novel inside of you.

Not long ago, our team came across an excellent book with examples of transitions, Russell Simmons' **Do You**.

Simmons speaks to his transition from a life in the streets to millionaire entrepreneur (Def Jam Records was his first venture).

Simmons was desperate to get into music. He just did not know how. So he offered to work for free handing out flyers for a man who created events for the music world.

"I didn't view handing out flyers as a demotion. I was happy to humble myself ... I was inspired by the music and wanted to be around it any way I could."

Simmons also tells the story of Kevin Liles (today Executive VP of Warner Music). One day Liles just showed up at Def Jam and pestered his way into an unpaid intern position.

"He worked harder than anyone in the company, always had a smile on his face, and never once mentioned money. Not once."

Liles made himself indispensable and his internship turned into a job. Within a few years he was the president of Def Jam.

FINDING YOUR PASSION, AND CREATING A LIVING AROUND IT, IS ONE OF LIFE'S CHALLENGES. THERE IS NO ONE WAY TO DO THAT. THE POINT IS TO KEEP TRYING.

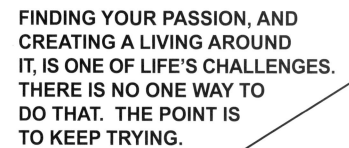

"Your work is to discover your work, and then with all your heart, give yourself to it."

Buddha

26

Billy's reading caused him to reflect upon those activities he most enjoys. He recalls that as a youngster he loved performing for his friends – doing magic tricks and cracking jokes. He thinks that may be a sign as to what he should be doing as an adult.

27

"If Jay worked as hard at his school work as he did at trying to be funny, he would do just fine."

Jay Leno's Fifth Grade Report Card

For many of us, childhood pursuits can be a sign. By reliving those activities that brought us joy as a child, we gain insight into our passions.

Some youngsters are fortunate and discover at a young age exactly what it is that they want to do with their lives. Let me give you two examples.

A few months ago I was speaking with Jim Nantz, lead sportscaster for CBS Sports and an Emmy winner for broadcast excellence. I have known Jim for a long time and he is a very gracious guy.

Holy cow! Eight years old!

And for many years Jim held onto his dream – doing everything in his power to turn it into a reality.

And when he was finally hired to broadcast college football for CBS Sports and sat in the CBS Studios in New York City … well, he can tell the story better than I can ...

34

"When I finally sat at the broadcast desk at the studios in New York, believe it or not, I felt like I had been there thousands of times before. After envisioning this experience for many years, I felt immediately comfortable."

35

Little Jim

"I have to keep my voice down as Palmer lines up his putt."

CBS SPORTS

Big Jim

36

I love the story of Jim Nantz. As an 8-year old he dreamed of broadcasting for CBS Sports and he never let go of his dream. Still, I believed that his experience had to be one in a million until a few weeks later, when I interviewed Brian Williams, the anchor of NBC News.

37

Brian Williams

"Brian, how did you happen to become an anchorman?"

"Well this may sound a bit ridiculous, but I was about 7 or 8 years old when I knew that I wanted to become a newscaster."

HOLY MOLY!

40

"You're kidding me…
7 or 8 years old?"

"No kidding… somehow I
just knew. Perhaps it was
because my mother would
not serve dinner until she
and my father were done
watching the news. As I
sat there hungry, I decided
what a dream job the news
anchors had."

41

By the way, like Jim Nantz, Brian Williams worked very hard to achieve success … years of hard work and even a bankruptcy when he could not make ends meet as a young broadcaster in Kansas. He finally got his break when, working at a low-level job for a TV station in Washington D.C., the station manager decided she liked him and gave him a shot on air.

Jim Nantz and Brian Williams were lucky … and they know it. To find your mission in life at an age like 8 is extraordinary. Most of us struggle – picking up signals piece by piece over time.

A friend of mine uses a cave analogy. He says that the search for the place where your passions and aptitudes intersect is like walking through a mostly dark cave with some shafts of light. We walk toward light, but most of the shafts end in narrow cracks, and so we turn in other directions. Eventually we find a source of light that gets brighter as it leads us toward the sunshine that will finally illuminate our exact journey.

"You pick up the pieces of treasure and trash, pain and pleasure, passions and disappointments, and you start throwing them in your bag, your big bag of experience. You do some dumb things that don't work out at all. You stumble excitedly on little gems that you never saw coming. And you stuff them all in your bag. You pursue the things you love and believe in. You cast off images of yourself that don't fit. And suddenly you look behind you and a pattern emerges.

There is nothing more beautiful than finding your course as you believe you bob aimlessly in the current. Wouldn't you know that your path was there all along, waiting for you to knock … like a photograph coming into focus."

Jodie Foster,
Commencement Speech, June, 2006

Young children are unvarnished by practicality. They are not worried about making money. They generally don't care what others think. They find the spot where they are happiest, and they live there in their imaginations.

Sometimes adults deem childhood ambitions as "unrealistic." But, like Jim Nantz and Brian Williams, those kids who stay the course can achieve great success:

Paul McCartney – turned down for the youth choir and frowned upon for poor grades, young Paul nevertheless kept playing his music.

Matt Groenig – incurred adult disapproval for spending too much time drawing cartoons; still, young Matt kept drawing right up to the day he created **The Simpsons**.

Barbra Streisand – teenage Barbra told her mother she wanted to be an actress and singer; her mother told her to take up secretarial work instead. But young Barbra would not listen (thank goodness for all of us Barbra fans).

49

50

51

52

59

60

Let me explain what I am trying to do.

Billy thinks he has a knack for making people laugh and maybe he does. But, that is far from enough. I want him to understand that tons of people have similar knacks, and that the journey from where he is today to the point where he makes a living in comedy is going to be long and challenging.

You see the reason many people give up on their dreams is that they **underestimate** how long and winding the road to success can be. I am trying to prepare Billy for the journey – by letting him know how many roadblocks and potholes and toll gates and wrong turns there will be ahead. By doing this I believe I can strengthen his fortitude to deal with challenges as they arise.

ANTICIPATE ADVERSITY

By expecting adversity, you prepare your mind. When it appears, you don't panic.

Instead, you say to yourself, "Aha, I did not know how or when but I knew there would be some difficult stretches. OK, adversity, bring it on!"

Of course, if adversity never shows up, that's good too.

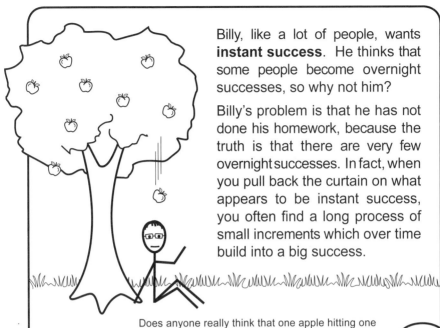

Billy, like a lot of people, wants **instant success**. He thinks that some people become overnight successes, so why not him?

Billy's problem is that he has not done his homework, because the truth is that there are very few overnight successes. In fact, when you pull back the curtain on what appears to be instant success, you often find a long process of small increments which over time build into a big success.

Does anyone really think that one apple hitting one head was the first time anyone thought about gravity?

Here is an excerpt from a great article by *New York Times* science columnist Janet Rae-Dupree. She researched the process of breakthroughs – instances when new ideas or discoveries seem to happen overnight.

Eureka! It Really Takes Years of Hard Work

"Innovation is a slow process of accretion, building small insight upon interesting fact upon tried-and-true process. Just as an oyster wraps layer upon layer of nacre atop an offending piece of sand, ultimately yielding a pearl, innovation percolates within hard work over time ... The myth of epiphany has a long history because it's appealing to believe that there is a short, simple reason that things happen. The story most often begins and ends with a determined, hard-working person trying, and failing, to find a solution to a given problem."

BEFORE YOU START OFF ON THE JOURNEY TO YOUR DREAMSCAPE – WHATEVER IT MIGHT BE – LEARN ABOUT OTHERS WHO HAVE ACCOMPLISHED WHAT YOU SEEK. IN MOST CASES YOU WILL LEARN ABOUT A LONG AND ARDUOUS CLIMB.

BY DOING THIS YOU BUFFER YOURSELF FOR THE DIFFICULTY OF YOUR OWN PASSAGE, AND YOU WILL THEREFORE BE LESS LIKELY TO LOSE HEART WHEN THE INEVITABLE WINDS START BLOWING RIGHT SMACK INTO YOUR FACE.

THOSE WHO ACCEPT RIGHT UP FRONT THE DIFFICULTY OF THE PASSAGE ARE LESS LIKELY TO QUIT WHEN THE GOING GETS TOUGH.

This point is emphasized in one of my favorite books, *The Road Less Traveled* by Dr. Scott Peck.

Here are the first two paragraphs of that book:

"Life is difficult.

This is a great truth, one of the greatest truths. It is a great truth because once we truly see this truth, we transcend it. Once we truly know that life is difficult – once we truly understand and accept it – then life is no longer difficult. Because once it is accepted, the fact that life is difficult no longer matters."

As said so well by Dr. Peck, whatever your ambition, the road to fulfillment will most likely not be quick or easy. You therefore need to prepare for a challenging trip. If you do that, then your trip will not be nearly as difficult as it might be … **and, more importantly, you are far less likely to stay down when you get knocked down … as you probably will.**

BILLY AND JIM HEAD OFF TO LUNCH

"Each of whom struggled for years before achieving success."

Stephen King: got so many rejection letters, he had to change the nail in his room (on which he hung these letters) to a large spike to hold his ever-increasing turn-downs … By the way, King's *On Writing* is a great book for aspiring writers.

J.K. Rowling: creator of the brilliant Harry Potter series, Ms. Rowling wrote for years whenever she could find moments of quiet time and space while caring for a child and living on welfare. But she could not get a publisher interested in her manuscript. Finally a small publisher took a chance on her, the president of which was reputed to have told her "Don't quit your day job!" (NOTE: Ms. Rowling had no day job.)

John Grisham: his legal thrillers have sold 250 million books. As a practicing lawyer, whenever he had a free 30 minutes he would hide away in the law library and write. It took Grisham years to find a publisher for his first manuscript (*A Time to Kill*).

Although I am speaking to Billy about his desire to make a living in comedy, his story is really a metaphor for any journey to the achievement of one's goals. I know a lot of successful people and not one of them had a pain-free trip to success.

My particular challenge with Billy is that he is underestimating the passage from where he is to where he wants to be. He believes that because he has an aptitude for making people laugh, his passage to success should be quick and easy.

"Billy, I am assuming that you have a great ability to make people laugh. But, even if that's so, it's a long journey to making a living as a comic."

"OK, OK ... I hear you, but some people make it, so why not me? Talent is the key and I know I have talent."

76

77

The Three Amigos

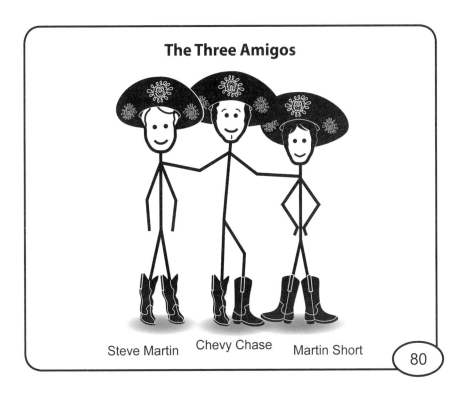

Steve Martin　　Chevy Chase　　Martin Short

"I love that movie, too. In fact, Steve Martin is my favorite comedian. Want to hear about his path to success?"

"Sure, why not?"

"Martin actually started performing when he was a young teen – working at Disneyland in a magic store where he would do tricks and try out jokes on customers. He graduated to doing kids parties and then when he was about twenty he tried to make it as a stand-up comedian."

"Want to guess how long it took him to achieve success?"

"Two years?"

"Good guess … how about 10 … and at several points along the way he almost quit."

"You're kidding."

What is it about being eight years old? Martin Short ... Jim Nantz ... Brian Williams ... maybe that is the age when a young person first begins to take notice of the world, and how he or she might fit into it.

... old, with a model airplane he received for Christmas.

Just for fun, want to guess who this 8 year old is? Here's a clue, he seems pretty pleased with his first toy airplane, and in 2009 he saved a lot of lives with his aviation skills.

Did you guess U.S. Airways Captain Chesley "Sully" Sullenberger who on January 15, 2009 guided his plane to a safe landing in the Hudson River, saving 155 lives?

"Adults are always asking kids what they want to be when they grow up because they are looking for ideas."

Paula
Poundstone

88

89

Billy just does not understand that 99% of the time success is the result of nothing more exotic than a lot of hard work and a specific mindset.

90

What kind of mindset?

1. Successful people understand that nothing good comes easy. As American Revolutionary Thomas Paine said in his hugely popular pamphlet *Common Sense*:

"That which we obtain too easily, we esteem too lightly. It is dearness only which gives everything its value. Heaven knows how to put a proper price on its goods."

Here's another way of saying the same thing:

"If it was easy, everyone would be doing it."

2. Successful people have no sense of entitlement or expectation that good things will just happen to them. They fully expect to have to fight for every foot of progress they make.

3. Successful people focus on the value they can bring to their endeavor. Billy seems to think that the world is waiting for his comedy. Successful people realize that they must always do their best to add value for their fans, customers, employers, stockholders or investors.

Here is an excerpt from an article about the kind of preparation Chris Rock does before he performs:

"For many months Rock has been piecing together his act in clubs ... Comedy bit by bit, he has built two hours of material one minute at a time, culling the belly laughs from the bombs ... 18 warm up shows at The Street Factory in New Jersey where the owner said 'he came out here and worked his material, over and over, cutting and trimming, until by the last show you could not believe what he had put together'."

**New York Times,
December 2007, David Carr**

"Billy, I need to make a very important point to you: what appears to be natural, effortless talent is most often the result of hours of hard work, practice and repetition. Let me tell you about two other great performers ... and what I learned from them."

"Have you ever heard of Penn and Teller?"

"The magicians?"

"Yes, the magicians ... well, I have always been interested in magic, and when Penn and Teller were just starting out I went to see them perform in a tiny theater in New York. Not only was their magic spectacular, but Penn Gillette was a brilliant comic ... ad lib after ad lib after ad lib. Walking out of the theater I remarked to my wife that Penn had a remarkable ability to think funny on his feet."

"See, you are making my point ... some people just have a natural talent."

101

"Not so quick, Billy. You see, about two weeks later I went back to the show, and I was shocked to discover that Penn's rapid-fire ad libs during the second show **were exactly the same as in the first** ... in other words, the whole thing was scripted and rehearsed."

Oy, here we go again, "talent, schmalent."

102

105

I had to get up and leave. Billy is as ready for *The Tonight Show* as I am. I'm trying to help him and he continues to look for short cuts. I don't know how to convince him that there just aren't any short cuts!

106

Billy is under the impression that he has some kind of natural talent for comedy. And, maybe he does. But aptitude is not enough for substantive achievement. In fact, aptitude is fourth or fifth on my list of the prerequisites for success … behind determination, courage, tenacity and patience.

Successful people understand that aptitude alone will never get you anywhere. Successful people are very hard workers. Even if they think they may have an aptitude or talent for a particular endeavor, they are not going to rely on that alone to take them to the finish line. They understand that the passage to success is one of clarity as to one's goals, hard work, and persistence.

This seems like an appropriate time to tell you about three recently published books – all very well written, informative and entertaining:

Outliers: The Story of Success, Malcolm Gladwell

Talent is Overrated, Geoff Colvin

The Talent Code: Greatness Isn't Born. It's Grown, Daniel Coyne

These three books contain amazing parallels in their analysis of the role that natural, inborn talent plays in one's success. All of these books reach a similar conclusion:

What appears as talent is almost always the result of years of hard work. What appears as effortless grace in performance, as excellence, is the result of years of practice, repetition and frustration.

Let me tell you a little bit about each book.

In **Outliers**, author Malcolm Gladwell concludes that success is far less about some kind of inborn ability and much more about environment, very hard work, or even good timing.

Gladwell references the research that a psychologist named K. Anders Ericsson did at a school for young, elite musicians:

"He and his colleagues could not find any 'naturals,' musicians who floated effortlessly to the top while practicing a fraction of the time their peers did. Nor could they find any 'grinds,' people who worked harder than everyone else, yet just didn't have what it takes to break into the top ranks ... the thing that distinguishes one performer from another is how hard he or she works. That's it. And what's more, the people at the top don't just work harder or even much harder than everyone else. They work much, MUCH harder."

I am a big fan of Professor Ericsson. Two years ago I was reading about his research and I just picked up the phone.

"Hello, Professor, my name is Jim Randel and I am writing a book on the subject of success. I wonder if you would be kind enough to discuss your views with me."

"Sure, Jim, I'm happy to do that."

"Thanks. Anyway, my question is what role you feel natural, genetically-coded talent plays in one's eventual success."

"Jim, our research indicates that one's mastery of a particular skill – what eventually leads to success at the chosen activity – is less about genetics and more about years and years of practice, repetition and a constant drive to improve. In fact, we believe that one can never really master a skill until he or she has invested at least 10,000 hours of practice."

10,000 HOURS!! Holy Cow!!

I need you to keep in mind, however, that Professor Ericsson was using that number as a baseline for the development of WORLD-CLASS EXCELLENCE.

Very few of us are looking for that level of achievement. Most of us just want to be the best we can be.

The "take away" from Ericsson's research is that most great achievers, the best of the best, reached the top not because of some natural gift, but rather because they expended hours and hours of practice and preparation that eventually manifests itself in a natural ease, grace, and excellence.

In **Outliers**, Gladwell researched athletics – where many people believe that natural, physical gifts are the key to success.

Gladwell wanted to get to the bottom of what factors lead to success in a really physical sport like hockey. So he traveled to the country where great stars are born and bred: Canada.

Gladwell dug deep and you will never guess what he found:

Gladwell discovered that success in Canada's hockey programs might be more about WHEN one was born than about WHAT physical traits one was born with!!

His research turned up an amazing fact:

It appears success in Canadian hockey is directly correlated to **the month** in which a youngster is born.

WHAT IS THIS ABOUT???

Gladwell did an analysis of top Canadian hockey players – young men who made high school or college all-star teams, and/or the National Hockey League.

And what he found was that those young men who were the most successful **were most often born in the first quarter of the year**.

In fact, the month of birth with the greatest number of star athletes was January. Second month of birth with the greatest number of star athletes? February. And then … well you guessed it, March.

I could never skate. I now believe it's because I was born in May.

Gladwell learned that youth hockey in Canada is tied to the calendar year so that all youngsters born in a given calendar year play together.

Gladwell realized that with youngsters – say beginning at age 6 – a matter of months in age can make a big difference in size and strength. What was happening in Canada was that the bigger and stronger boys at age 6 were getting more attention, more coaching and more playing time. As a result, the 6 year olds who were bigger and stronger – simply because they were born earlier in the calendar year – BECAME the best hockey players BECAUSE OF the increased attention paid to them...and not due to some genetic blessing.

NOTE: If a youngster born on December 31st had been a bit stubborn such that he was born on January 1st instead of December 31st, he would have been competing against youngsters born up to 12 months later. He would have likely been bigger and stronger than they were and, as a result, received a lot more attention and coaching ... perhaps leading to hockey greatness.

JUST FOR FUN I GOOGLED MY FAVORITE HOCKEY PLAYER ...

CANADIAN WAYNE GRETZKY.

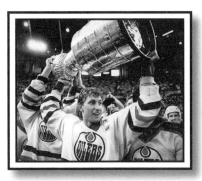

BIRTHDATE: JANUARY 26, 1961.

Gladwell wanted to test his theory elsewhere in the world, so he researched European soccer teams where, like Canadian youth hockey, the youth programs are run on a calendar year.

As an example, Gladwell obtained the roster for the 2007 Czechoslovakian National Junior Team that made the World Cup (junior) Finals.

There were 21 superb athletes on that team. Guess how many were born **in the first three months of the year?**

A)   10 (47%)
B)   12 (57%)
C)   14 (67%)
D)   16 (77%)

Yes, D is correct! 77% or 16 out of 21 team members were born in the first three months of the year!!

"The closer psychologists looked at the careers of the gifted, the smaller the role innate talent seems to play..."

Outliers, Malcolm Gladwell

In Geoff Colvin's well-researched book, **Talent is Overrated,** he reaches conclusions very similar to those of Malcolm Gladwell: that success in a particular endeavor is usually the result of years of development and practice … and not some unique gift or aptitude.

"Research doesn't support the view that extraordinary natural general abilities – as distinct from developed abilities – are necessary for high achievement. … (Findings on achievement) explicitly rejected the 'you've-got-it-or-you-don't' view. It explained high achievement without the concept of talent playing any role."

123

Colvin does not believe that even braininess – raw intelligence – is much of a predictor for success.

"In a wide range of fields, including business, the connection between general intelligence and specific abilities is weak and in some cases nonexistent."

124

Warren Buffet recently said the same thing:

"If you have an IQ of 150, good for you. But, I suggest you sell about 30 points. You don't need to be that smart."

Colvin brings up another point relative to the attainment of excellence in performance.

Given that the key to success with and mastery of a particular skill is lots of practice and repetition, Colvin asks the questions: "What kind of practice ... **will any practice do?**"

And the answer is a resounding "NO." Excellence does not come from just any practice. Excellence comes from "deliberate practice" – the process of analyzing and identifying what you are **not** good at – and working at that.

In other words, in order to develop real excellence, you need to work at the edges of your current aptitude – areas where you struggle.

As said by Coach John Wooden (famous basketball coach):

"Practice does not make perfect ... perfect practice makes perfect."

Coach Wooden's point is the same as Geoff Colvin's: to be great, you need to practice those skills you are not already good at.

Geoff Colvin's book really got me thinking when he recounted the story of the amazing Polgar family.

Laszlo Polgar, a psychologist living in Hungary during the 1960's, believed that talent is made, not born. And he decided to prove it with a very unusual experiment.

Laszlo decided to create a family. He would be the father and he would advertise for a wife. They would have children and bring up their children to be champions in a field that neither he nor his wife had any aptitude for.

People in Hungary loved the game of chess. And there were many Hungarian chess grand masters, men who reached the pinnacle of the chess world with their amazing talent for the game.

All these grand masters were believed to have exceptional intelligence and mental quickness, a unique aptitude for thinking many moves ahead, and a rare ability to focus for long periods of time while under pressure.

Laszlo finds a wife.

A schoolteacher named Klara answered Laszlo's advertisement and agreed to the terms of his experiment: they would have children and since neither Laszlo nor Klara was an accomplished chess player, they would select chess as the sport in which they would attempt to create champions.

Things became even more interesting when Klara gave birth to three girls – I mean everyone knew that women did not have the right stuff to be grand masters.

Laszlo and Klara home schooled their three daughters, including intensive training in chess. Soon the girls were entering competitions.

Their first daughter became the first female grand master ever.

Their second daughter became the youngest grand master ever – MALE OR FEMALE – younger even than the American male prodigy, Bobby Fischer.

Their third daughter is currently the #1 ranked woman player in the world.

"There was no reason to suppose that Laszlo or Klara passed on any innate chess ability to their daughters; Laszlo was only a mediocre player, and Klara had demonstrated no chess ability at all. The story of the Polgars illustrates how the principles of deliberate practice, when carried to an extraordinary level, produce extraordinary achievement."

Talent is Overrated

I was fascinated by the story of the little Polgar girls. Laszlo and Klara wanted to make a point, and they did.

While I was reading it, I wondered to myself what would have happened if Laszlo and Klara had decided to try to make their daughters into great athletes. I wondered whether the Polgar girls could have excelled, for example, in track and field – where success would seem to be tied to innate abilities to run and jump.

So, I picked up the phone and called a long-time friend of mine, Dwight Stones – one of America's greatest high jumpers.

Dwight is a four-time Olympian and ten-time world record holder. He is tall and lean.

136

137

Dwight did say that his height "got him in the door," and there are, of course, some activities where specific physical attributes are required. Basketball, for one. Certainly no short person is going to succeed at basketball.

138

THEN AGAIN, THERE ALWAYS SEEM TO BE EXCEPTIONS.

Muggsy Bogues was the 12th player selected in the first round of the 1987 NBA draft. He is 5'3" tall and he played in the NBA for 14 years!!

139

OK, so maybe the basketball height thing doesn't always hold true, but I don't think SHAQ is ever going to make it as a jockey.

140

High jumper Dwight Stones was no help with my question:

Suppose Laszlo and Klara Polgar had decided to put their prodigious efforts into making their 3 daughters track and field athletes … would they have become world class?

141

Here is my take on my own question: I believe that some people have a genetic predisposition for certain activities. Just because Laszlo and Klara Polgar were not chess players does not mean that their daughters were not born with some kind of an instinct for the game. (Note that Laszlo was a psychologist and Klara was a school teacher.)

Still, this much I am sure about: an inborn trait will never mature into excellence without lots of hard work, practice and repetition, determination and desire, and persistence.

The Polgar experiment made me think about Tiger Woods.

When Tiger was born, his father, Earl, had retired from the Army, had three grown children from a prior marriage and a stay-at-home wife. And Earl and his wife decided to make Tiger their priority.

Earl had not played golf as a young man but as an adult became fanatic about the sport. When Tiger was ten months old Earl would set up his high chair in their garage while Earl hit golf balls into a net.

And Tiger sat there and took it all in.

By the time Tiger was two years old, Earl and Tiger were visiting golf courses and playing together regularly!

Tiger was even a bit of a celebrity.

A two-year-old old Tiger showing his skills on national TV.

And today, of course, Tiger is perhaps the greatest golfer that has ever lived.

What is interesting about Tiger's story is that neither he nor his father have suggested that Tiger was born with a gift for golf.

Trying to explain his early interest in the game, Tiger has not invoked some kind of natural attraction. Rather he has written: "golf for me was an apparent attempt to emulate the person I looked up to more than anyone: my father."

146

Asked to explain Tiger's incredible success, father and son always gave the same response:

HARD WORK ... VERY, VERY HARD WORK.

147

I wonder what would have happened if Earl Woods decided that the young Tiger should play chess instead of golf?

Would Tiger have gravitated to golf nevertheless?

Would Tiger Woods be a grand chess master today?

And I have other questions:

Can anyone with a firm enough resolve will themselves to greatness whatever the endeavor?

I think that the answer has to be "no." Not every youngster who gravitates to the game of golf will win a major championship. Not every hard-working young singer will win *American Idol*. Not every ambitious acting student will ever hold an Academy Award.

But (and it is a very important "but") without giving your chosen activity all that you have, you will never know how far you can go.

"(Do positive thinkers believe) that anyone with proper motivation or education can become Einstein or Beethoven? No, but they believe that a person's true potential is unknown (and unknowable); that it's impossible to foresee what can be accomplished (until one has invested) years of passion, toil, and training."

Mindset: How We Can Learn to Fulfill our Potential,
Carol Dweck

The author of the above quote, Dr. Carol Dweck, is a professor of psychology at Stanford University.

Her view is that achievement is about the type of attitude one brings to adversity and challenge. People with what Dr. Dweck calls a "growth mindset" operate under the belief that basic qualities (talent) can be learned and cultivated through effort.

"Although people may differ in every which way ... everyone can grow and change through application and experience."

I particularly like this quote:

"Just because some people can do something with little or no training, it doesn't mean that others can't do it (and sometimes do it better) with training."

LET'S SUMMARIZE WHAT WE HAVE LEARNED SO FAR FROM GLADWELL, COLVIN AND DWECK:

There are very few limits on what each of us can accomplish. If we really really want something, we have a shot at getting it – whatever our inborn aptitudes, smarts or physical make-up.

"Compared to what we ought to be, we are only half awake. We are making use of only a small part of our physical and mental resources. Stating the thing broadly, the human individual lives far within his limits. We all have reservoirs of energy and genius to draw upon of which we do not dream."

Dr. William James
Famous American Psychologist

LAST BUT NOT LEAST, DANIEL COYNE'S GREAT BOOK ON SUCCESS, ***THE TALENT CODE***, PROVIDES ADDITIONAL INSIGHT INTO THE QUEST FOR EXCELLENCE ... AND FROM EXCELLENCE TO SUCCESS.

Coyne explains why the prerequisite to mastery is lots of practice.

Coyne tells us about MYELIN (rhymes with violin), a microscopic substance that wraps itself around nerve fibers to increase their effectiveness.

Let's take a minute to discuss the human body.

When you decide to move, you send a signal from your brain to a muscle. This signal is transmitted along nerve fibers. The better your nerve fibers work, the more likely that the exact action you want will occur.

Your nerve fibers send and receive electrical signals indicating your desired actions. The goal is to have the electrical signal transmitted as quickly and efficiently as possible so that **exactly** what you want to have happen will, in fact, happen.

The way to make your nerve fibers work their best is to have them wrapped in myelin because myelin improves the conductivity of nerve cells, i.e. their ability to send and receive electrical signals.

So how do you get a lot of myelin wrapped around your nerve fibers?

Well, here is the good part: YOU USE YOUR NERVE FIBERS AS MUCH AS POSSIBLE.

Myelin is produced when a nerve fiber fires, i.e., sends out electrical signals. So, the more you use that nerve fiber, the more myelin is produced and the more efficiently your nerves send and receive electrical signals.

Therefore, by practicing over and over and over, you are using nerves, producing myelin, improving the conductivity of your nerves because of the increased myelin ... and getting increasingly skillful at whatever you are trying to do!!

"Skill therefore is simply the product of myelin wrapping itself around nerve fibers."

The Talent Code

You may have heard people speak about muscle memory.

Muscle memory, or the retaining of information about specific movements, is really about myelin. The more you do something, the more myelin you produce around the engaged nerve fibers, and the better you become at it.

Or, if you prefer, the better your muscles become at replicating the exact action you desire.

Is the production of myelin also a factor in developing skillfulness in non-physical activities like chess?

The functioning of the brain is still, to a large degree, a mystery to scientists so I cannot say for sure.

But, this much we know – the more people perform mental activities (memory tests, crossword puzzles, chess and brain teasers), the better they get at them.

So, no matter how you slice it, practice – especially at the edges of your present ability – leads to improvement at whatever you do. Conversely, without that practice, your level of proficiency can decline.

"When I miss one day of practice, no one can tell but me.

When I miss two days of practice, my wife can tell.

When I miss three days of practice, my audience can tell."

Vladimir Horowitz,
concert pianist

Reading **The Talent Code** I wondered to myself about the limits of myelin creation.

For years I have been a recreational jogger. Lately I have been thinking of entering a marathon. My goal will be to finish in a respectable time. I'll try my best but a person can't just will himself to run fast ... or can he?

Author Daniel Coyne wondered the same thing one day as he watched his four children chasing each other around his backyard.

Coyne has four children, the youngest of whom is his daughter Zoe. One day he was sitting outside and he noticed that Zoe could easily outrun her older siblings. Zoe was just a super speedy kid. And that got Coyne thinking.

"Foot speed has got to be some kind of natural ability," he thought to himself. The explanation for Zoe's speediness could not be simply that she happened to run a lot, and as a result developed more myelin around her nerve fibers. Or could it?

Then Coyne thought about why Zoe might want to run more than her siblings. Well, as the youngest she was always trying to keep up with them. And perhaps at times even trying to keep away from them.

But if that were the case, then the youngest child in a birth order would always be the fastest runner in the family, since he or she would have the greatest incentive to keep up with (or away from) older, stronger siblings.

On its face, that idea seems absurd. Or does it??

Coyne wondered whether Zoe's speediness was just an aberration in his family.

So, he decided to look at the families of some really really fast runners: world record holders.

Coyne obtained a list of the last ten world record holders' in the men's 100 meter dash.

He then obtained information about the world record holder's siblings and birth order.

And what he found was incredible!!

The average number of children in the world record holder's families was 4.6.

The world record holder's average birth order was 4.0.

In other words, the world record holder was almost always the youngest child!!

"(The result of our study) strikes us as surprising because speed looks like a gift. It feels like a gift. And yet this pattern suggests that speed is not purely a gift but a skill that grows through deep practice ... ignited by primal cues."

The Talent Code

I'd like to tell you about three superb runners, because in a way each one makes the point that success as an athlete is as much a matter of **one's mind** as one's body. And, to extend the point, that any success – of whatever kind – is more about the strength of your mind, i.e., your will, than the strength of your natural talent or intellect.

First, I need to tell you about Glenn Cunningham.

In 1917 eight-year-old Glenn Cunningham (the youngest of two boys) was badly burned in a fire. The doctors advised his parents that Glenn would never walk again and to prevent infection, recommended amputation of his legs.

But young Glenn would just not cooperate. He fought the amputation and the doctors relented.

Two years later Glenn was walking – quite unsteady to be sure – but he got up, out of his wheelchair.

Fifteen years later, in 1934, Glenn Cunningham broke the world record for the mile run.

Twenty years later another world record in the mile run was shattered when Roger Bannister did the impossible.

In 1954, track and field experts were united on one point of view: **no one would ever run the mile in under four minutes**.

This was simple physiology. The human heart-lung capacity could not withstand the kind of stress that would occur if someone ran that fast. In fact, some doctors maintained that anyone who broke the four-minute barrier would probably die shortly thereafter as his lungs would most likely explode.

Until, that is, Roger Bannister (the youngest of two children) ran the mile in 3:59.4 in May, 1954.

Now here is the interesting part. About a month later, another runner broke Bannister's record – running the mile in 3:57.9. And within a few years the four minute barrier was just a silly idea as runners from all over the world were running miles under 4 minutes.

Now did all these sub-four-minute milers suddenly gain new **physical** ability – ability that allowed them to shave seconds off their best time? Or, could it have been instead that once the **mental barrier** of 4 minutes was erased from their mind, the mind took over – with improved performance the result?

By the way, today the world record for the mile run is 3:43.13!!

Roger Bannister

Finally, I want to tell you what might be the most amazing athletic story of all.

Wilma Rudolph was born prematurely in 1940. She weighed 4.5 pounds. (By the way, she was the 20th of 22 children!)

As an infant, she contracted polio and wore a brace on her twisted leg for the first twelve years of her life. She was a sickly child who also suffered suffered from scarlet fever and whooping cough.

Her doctors said she would never walk without crutches but her mother said that she would. Wilma chose to believe her mother.

In 1960 Wilma Rudolph won three gold medals in the Rome Olympics – including the 100 meter dash.

Here are Ms. Rudolph's words which should be inspiration for those of us laboring with many fewer challenges than young Wilma faced:

"Never underestimate the power of dreams and the influence of the human spirit. We are all the same in this notion: the potential for greatness lives within each of us."

Wilma Rudolph

What can we learn from these stories?

We should learn that the mind is tremendously powerful. That whatever you seek, if you have a will to succeed, a determination that cannot be defeated, a steely refusal to quit in the face of adversity – well, then almost anything is possible.

> *"There are those who think they can … and those who think they can't … and both are right."*
>
> *Anonymous*

A STRONG MIND IS YOUR BEST FRIEND.

All of the successful people I know have strong minds. I don't mean brainy. Some are smart and some of average intelligence. But what they all have is the ability to use their mind to their advantage.

In another of our books (**The Skinny on Willpower**) I talk about mental discipline. Let me summarize for you some of the highlights:

1. The thoughts floating around in your head jump in and out. They are the result of many events and stimuli in your life that have occurred up to this minute. They may or may not be conducive to your success.

2. The good news is that you are free to choose which thoughts you want. As Eckhart Tolle teaches in **The Power of Now**, you are not your thoughts. You are the observer of your thoughts. In recognizing this, "thought loses its power over you … because you are no longer energizing the mind through identification with it. This is the beginning of the end of involuntary and compulsive thinking."

3. Napoleon Hill (**Think & Grow Rich**) suggests that you think of your thoughts as "things" – tangible objects that you can eject from or insert into your consciousness as you see fit. In doing so, you retain the thoughts that foster your success and evict those that don't.

4. All of our actions (and inactions) are controlled by our thoughts. Often we are victim to fears that are unrealistic and destructive. By increasing your awareness of those thoughts and anxieties which control your decisions, you are better positioned to make well-reasoned choices.

5. Successful people attempt to master their thoughts: (i) they do not let irrational anxieties control their actions (or inactions), (ii) they do not allow ego or a sense of entitlement interfere with their best efforts, (iii) they do not let an event of failure remain in their mind for long – immediately it becomes "yesterday's news," (iv) they do not abide by thoughts of complacency, (v) they do not permit ideas of procrastination, (vi) they do not let criticism and feelings of inadequacy linger in their mind, (vii) they do not feel sorry for themselves no matter what happens, (viii) they do not get down on themselves – they understand that a climb up the ladder of success can be lonely at times and they give themselves credit for trying, (ix) they develop focusing skills – the ability to fill their mind with clear, dominating thoughts to the exclusion of all else, and (x) they develop the mental fortitude to persist in the severe headwinds.

Here is one of the most important points in this book:

Mental fortitude is an acquired skill.

Every single one of you who ever touch this book can develop the strength of mind to improve the likelihood of success in your chosen endeavor. You can learn to control your thoughts.

If you are interested in learning more about mind control, see the bibliography at the end of this book.

Strength of Mind

As you may know, one of the most successful self-improvement books of the last 50 years is Stephen Covey's *The Seven Habits of Highly Successful People.*

In this book Covey talks about mental fortitude, what he describes as "response – ability," the ability to choose your response to whatever is happening around you.

"Highly proactive people ... do not blame circumstances, conditions or conditioning for their behavior. Their behavior is the product of their own conscious choice ... The difference between people who exercise (this) initiative and those who don't is literally the difference between night and day. I'm not talking about a 25 to 50 percent difference in effectiveness, I'm talking about a 5000-plus percent difference!"

184

185

"I know, but 25 years old. Your opponent is going to call you inexperienced and naïve."

"He will probably do that and, truthfully this whole idea petrifies me, but I can't let that stop me."

Good for Beth! It sounds like she is going to declare her candidacy!

So many people leave their dreams on the table – often due to fear. Fear of failure… fear of looking stupid … fear of the unknown.

Hey, there are no guarantees in life. Once you reach for your dreams, you may embarrass yourself, you may get knocked down, you will incur setbacks.

But, unless you get in the game, there is a 100% guarantee that your dreams will never come true.

FEAR + INACTION = REGRET

In an article entitled *"The Experience of Regret: What, When and Why?"* published by the American Psychological Association, the authors summarize studies that ask people what they would do differently if they could live their lives over.

By a margin of 4 to 1, the respondents regretted INACTION over action. In other words, 4 out of 5 people regretted not what they did … **but what they did not do!**

"Tell me, what is it you plan to do with your one wild and precious life?"

The Summer Day, Mary Oliver
Pulitzer Prize Winner for Poetry

Beth is struggling a bit. She has always been interested in politics but she is nervous now that it may be a reality. Perhaps I can help.

Am I crazy considering a run for Town Council? I wonder if any candidate ever got no votes?

"Knock, knock. May I come in?"

194

195

"I know … I have not even declared, and already I'm not sleeping well."

"Well, usually it's the deliberation which creates the most anxiety. Once you take the first step forward, things are often less stressful."

196

"I hope you are right. I realize that the odds are against me. I just don't want to fail miserably."

"Beth, I want to make a really important point to you … even if you do fail, and miserably, you are a winner because you took a step toward your dreamscape. The key to achievement is to see failure as just a stepping stone to success. People of great achievement recognize that failure is simply a part of the process to success."

197

198

199

"See if you can guess who this is:

At age 21 he failed in business.

At age 23 he was defeated in an election for state legislature.

At age 24 his new business failed.

At age 26 he was overwhelmed with grief when his fiancée died.

At age 27 he had a nervous breakdown.

At age 34 he was defeated in an election for the U.S. Congress.

At age 36 he was again defeated in an election for the U.S. Congress.

At age 45 he was defeated in an election for the U.S. Senate.

At age 49 he was again defeated in an election for U.S. Senate."

"Success is the ability to go from failure to failure without the loss of enthusiasm."

Winston Churchill

"And by the way, if your opponent makes an issue of your age …
well, let me tell you a story about Ronald Reagan."

When Ronald Reagan ran for President in 1984 (second term), he was 74 years old and many commentators suggested that he was too old to be President. His opponent for the Presidency was a much younger Walter Mondale (age 56).

Reagan was elected in a landslide and at the end of his second term, he left office with one of the highest approval ratings of any modern-day president.

Beth is at an important crossroads in her life. She has always been interested in politics but, like anyone who ventures into something new, she is feeling fear and doubt. That is normal. Ideas and dreams are safe when they reside only in your mind. Bringing them out into the light of day is scary.

"When you are a Bear of Very Little Brain, and you Think of Things, you find sometimes that a Thing which seemed very Thingish inside you is quite different when it gets out into the open and has other people looking at it."

Winnie the Pooh

OFTEN, THE BEST ANTIDOTE FOR FEAR AND DOUBT IS THAT FIRST STEP FORWARD.

"The journey of a thousand miles begins with a first step."

Lao-Tzu

Successful people take action. They aren't impulsive but they know that sooner or later as Einstein said, "nothing happens until something moves."

In our studies of successful individuals, we found many who took action in the pursuit of their dreams **even though** by all rights, they had no business expecting success. In some cases, they just didn't know any better.

SILLY BOYS

Homer Hickam grew up in Coalwood, West Virginia in the 1950's. Coalwood was a mining town.

Homer did not have much going for him. In high school he was not a particularly good student. Nor was he an athlete. Not much seemed to energize him … until one night in 1957 when he was listening to the radio, and heard the "Beep – Beep – Beep" of the Russian satellite, Sputnik.

You see in the 1950's, the United States and Russia were in a competition to be the first country to send a satellite into space. And Russia won when it launched Sputnik into space in October of 1957. Americans were shocked and mounted a national effort to catch the Russians.

And for whatever reason, young Homer felt he could help – notwithstanding the fact that he had no money, had no background in science, and had no contacts or family who could assist him. Still, he was determined.

Homer and his pals decided to form their own space agency. So, they formed the Big Creek Missile Agency (not exactly NASA) in an attempt to send "rockets" into space. These rockets were cylindrical metal tubes stuffed with fire crackers. Their experiments were humorous if nothing else.

But the boys persisted. They never got into space of course but they did win a science fair for their efforts. This win helped Homer get a scholarship to college where he studied engineering. After college he got a job with NASA.

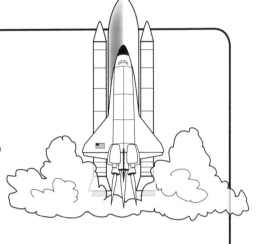

In a touching sequel to the story of Homer and his pals' efforts, Homer recounts how many years later an astronaut he knew agreed to take one of the boys' "nose cones" into space with him.

"As I watched the great ship blast off from the Cape Canaveral pad, I was filled with pride and happiness: the Big Creek Missile Agency was finally going into space."

Homer and his friends never actually launched a rocket into outer space.

But, by taking action – by pursuing something they felt strongly about – a piece of one of their rockets actually made it into space years later.

The point is (forgive the metaphor), you just never know how high you can go unless you take action. Inaction is an absolute game stopper. Game over. Dreams over.

*FOR A HEART-WARMING STORY OF YOUTHFUL ENTHUSIASM AND NAIVETE, YOU MIGHT WANT TO READ HOMER HICKHAM'S BIOGRAPHY, **ROCKET BOYS**.*

As illustrated by Homer Hickham and his buddies, sometimes youthful enthusiasm is amazing. That's because young people have not yet been dissuaded by life's naysayers.

As another example, I'd like to tell you about Richard Branson, the British entrepreneur (billionaire) who started Virgin Music, then Virgin Airlines and a whole slew of other Virgin businesses.

By the way, can you guess why he selected the name "Virgin?" Because, as Richard explained, he knew so little about business when he started his music company, no other name seemed appropriate.

SHEER ABSURDITY

Richard Branson grew up poor in the English countryside. He was dyslexic and never did well in school.

"Dyslexia wasn't deemed a problem in these days, or, put more accurately, it was a problem only if you were dyslexic yourself. Since nobody had ever heard of dyslexia, being unable to read, write or spell just meant to the rest of the class and teachers that you were either stupid or lazy."

Losing My Virginity, Richard Branson

Not exactly the lad odds-makers would select to become one of England's most famous entrepreneurs. But, Branson had a "problem." **He just did not realize he had no chance at success**.

And so, at age 15 he started a magazine (which led him to the music business) and before he even had one issue printed, he began selling advertising space to local businesses.

"My schoolwork was going from bad to worse ... had I been five or six years older, the sheer absurdity of trying to sell advertising to major companies in a magazine that did not yet exist and that was edited by two fifteen-year-old schoolboys, would have prevented me from picking up the phone at all. But I was too young to contemplate failure."

Branson was too young to understand the **sheer absurdity** of what he was doing!

So he just took action and started selling ad space. Then, he created a magazine. Then, a little business selling records. Then a big music business. Then, an airline.

> *"Many a false step is taken by just standing still."*
>
> **Anonymous**

In other words, sometimes you just have to go for it. Or, as the powerful Nike slogan suggests:

JUST DO IT!!

By the way, if you want to read about another billionaire entrepreneur, pick up the book, *Just Do It,* about Nike founder Phil Knight. One day Mr. Knight made a "nutty" decision to quit his job as an accountant and, **"just do it"** when he started selling running shoes out of the trunk of his car.

> *"The desire for safety stands against every great and noble enterprise."*
>
> **Tacitus, Historian of the Roman Empire**

219

LET'S CHECK BACK WITH BETH

220

"Well, Beth, not what you hoped but a good first step."

"You know what, Jim… you can be aggravating."

"Don't you ever just shut up?"

223

224

We are at a critical juncture in this book. Beth, one of our main characters, has just suffered a very painful setback and is thinking about giving up on her dream of public service and politics.

Somehow I have to explain to her that every successful person I know, no exceptions, has experienced painful setbacks in his or her journey to success. It is almost as if adversity is a "rite of passage."

If I were to point to one dominant characteristic of all the successful people I know, it would be an absolute refusal to quit – a steely persistence no matter what.

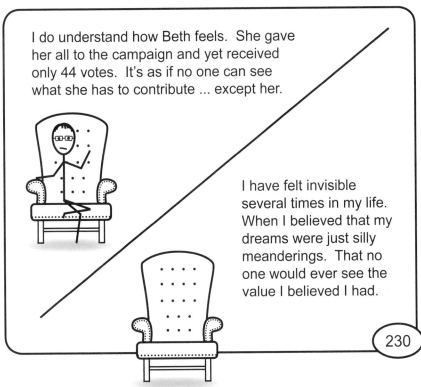

Often the drive for success is lonely.

Even people who love you have their own dreams. They want you to realize your goals, of course, but they are focused on their goals. Therefore, it is you – and you alone – who must fuel your quest for the life you want.

My office borders on a golf course and I have a great view of the golfers outside my window. There is one young golfer who practices every day. He is there early every morning, and then again at dusk.

This young man, trying to achieve excellence and success in his field, labors alone. Sometimes it rains but he is still there. Sometimes it is cold and windy. But he is there.

To me, this young man is what success is about. In his mind he sees a chance at greatness. Perhaps no one else believes in him. Maybe to the rest of the world he is invisible **but in his mind, there is a crystal clear image of him winning a championship**. That image is what keeps him going – no matter how lonely he may get.

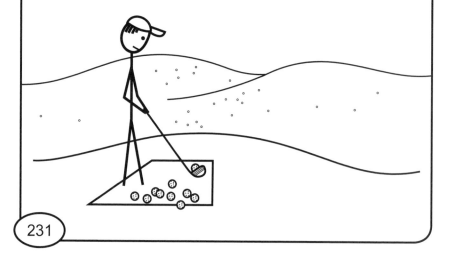

Like the young golfer I see out my window, you need to hang onto your dreams like a dog on a bone. Many of today's success stories had to conquer doubt and fear … and in some cases, very inauspicious beginnings.

FUTURE HALL OF FAMER DEREK JETER BATTED .202 HIS FIRST SEASON IN THE MINORS ... AND MADE 56 ERRORS.

"I was about eight years old as I walked into my parents' bedroom. I announced I was going to play for the Yankees."

"(My first game as a pro) was a double-header. I went 0 for 7 and struck out five times. I also made a throwing error … caused us to lose the game. … I hadn't imagined crying in my hotel room night after night because I was playing so poorly. I had my doubts. I felt overwhelmed."

"I'm the same skinny kid from Kalamazoo who bounced a ball off the side of my house and swung a bat every day in my garage. … I overcame challenges. I made it to the majors and made it as the shortstop for the Yankees. You have to make sure you don't treat your dreams like they are ONLY dreams. You have to feel that they can become realities.".

The Life You Imagine,
Derek Jeter

"Jim, maybe I'm just not cut out for politics. Maybe I'm not smart enough, articulate enough, or charismatic enough."

"Beth, I won't give you my 'talent, schmalent' speech, but I do want to suggest that the number one determinant of success in any endeavor is persistence."

233

"I have heard the 'talent schmalent' speech from Billy… I just don't know what to believe… I look at great speakers like Bill Clinton and Barack Obama and know I can never do what they do… I get nervous speaking in front of *ten* people."

"Beth, you never know what you can do until you push yourself. Clinton and Obama were not always great public speakers. Both of them had years of practice before you ever heard of them."

234

"But they are so natural … so smooth, so polished."

"Yes, they are … that is true. But, excellence comes with time in almost any endeavor. Did you know that the man considered to be the greatest orator ever, Demosthenes, is believed to have practiced speaking with pebbles in his mouth to work on his projection and articulation."

"Wow, pebbles in his mouth. I guess he was really determined to be the best orator around."

"I guess he was. Speaking of that, Beth, do you want to be President of the United States?"

237

238

241

242

Anyway, the **Encyclopedia Britannica** plays a role in the study I want to tell you about.

Back in the 1960's a psychologist by the name of Martin Eisenstadt wanted to try to understand UBER-success. What was at the root of the "rage to master?" What was it that drove some people to achieve a level of success far beyond what most of us even aim for.

First, Eisenstadt needed to identify UBER-successful people and what he did was go to his 30-volume **Encyclopedia Britannica** and count the number of people who were famous enough to receive more than a half page reference in the **Encyclopedia**.

He figured that anyone getting that much "ink" was some kind of super-succeeder. His approach was arbitrary, of course, but as good a system as any.

His list of super-succeeders was comprised of 573 famous folks ranging from Homer to John F. Kennedy.

As a next step, Eisenstadt had to dig into these people's lives to try to find a common thread.

And to his surprise, the commonality he found was that a large percentage of the 573 notables were quite young when one or both of their parents died. On average, the famous achievers were 13 years old when one of their parents died.

Then Eisenstadt looked at control groups of 573 randomly selected people and obtained information about their ages when a parent died. On average, in the control groups the members were 19 years old when they lost a parent.

"So your point is that the death of a young person's parent propels him or her to achieve greatness in some endeavor?"

"This stuff is not scientific Beth, but yes, I believe that is one factor. I feel that many superstars are driven by a sense of loss, maybe a death or a divorce or an unhappy childhood. Perhaps some kind of poor self-image. Some need to compensate."

245

"Wow… how does your theory apply to say, Presidents Clinton and Obama?"

"As it happens, Clinton's father actually died before baby Bill was born, and Obama's father left young Barack and his mother when the future President was just three years old."

246

"Well how about my personal hero, Oprah Winfrey?"

"Oprah has been very forthcoming about her childhood. She was raised by her grandmother. She was sexually abused at a young age. As a teenager, she became pregnant and gave birth to a baby, who died shortly thereafter. I would guess these events are part of the fuel that drove Oprah to her tremendous success."

247

"Wow."

"By the way, Beth, are both of your parents still alive?"

248

While Beth is thinking things over, I have some questions for you: Are you someone with a "rage to master?" Do you have a burning desire to succeed? Do you want to be the best of the best at what you do? Do you want to be President of the United States?

There are no right or wrong answers of course. I am just trying to get you to review your ambitions. Some people are quite happy stepping off the ladder to success after just a few rungs. Others won't be happy unless they reach the top.

HERE IS WHAT WORKS FOR ME:

1. Exercise

I accomplish two things with a regular program of exercise. First, I increase my energy. To a large degree success is about an application of energy at the right time and places. Second, I find that exercise clears my head and tamps down my anxiety.

2. Routine and Habit

I try to keep to a regular routine no matter what is going on in my life. When I am having a series of bad days – and the world seems to be falling apart – I find serenity in the predictability of certain events: a shower in the morning, reading the newspaper with breakfast, a quiet time before bed to give thanks. Recently I read a book by Twyla Tharp, a great choreographer, and learned that Ms. Tharp also relied on routine to get her through bad stretches:

> *"My support comes from my routine, my sustenance from my rituals of self-reliance."*

> *The Creative Habit*

3. My Mantra

When I am in a bad place, suffering with some problem as the world seems to be spinning out of control, I repeat a mantra that has worked for me on many prior occasions: "That which does not kill me makes me stronger." Those words are, of course, from the philosopher Goethe, for which I thank him, because when I repeat them over and over, they seem to calm my angst and build my spirit.

"About twenty years ago, I was buying real estate like it was going out of style. I had a few very successful deals and I got a big head. I started to think that I had a golden touch, and I bought a building which I shouldn't have.

"It was a factory building on about ten acres in Shelton, Connecticut. The building was leased for one year and during that period all the expenses of ownership were covered. My goal within that first year was to get the property rezoned, knock down the factory, and build a small shopping center.

"I thought I had all the bases covered, and my application for a rezoning was successful. But, before I even stopped patting myself on the back, the property owner across the street sued me.

"He did not want more retail in Shelton and so he challenged the rezoning as being unlawful."

"Are you Jim Randel?
You are being sued."

"Is this a joke?"

My inflated ego had ignored the possibility that someone might fight the rezone, and a challenge to a rezoning can be a real mess. At this point I did not know if my property was approved for retail or not. So, I could not begin development. I was stuck, and since a year had almost gone by, the tenant in the building was about to leave. As a result, my carrying costs were about to go from zero to $50,000 per month ... and I was about to be in serious trouble.

HERE IS WHAT CALVIN COOLIDGE SAID:

"Nothing can take the place of persistence.

Talent will not; nothing is more common than unsuccessful men with talent.

Genius will not; unrewarded genius is almost a proverb.

Education will not; the world is full of educated derelicts.

Persistence and determination are omnipotent.

The slogan 'PRESS ON' has solved and always will solve the problems of the human race."

Just for fun, see if you can pick out the photo of Calvin Coolidge, the 30th President of the United States.

See last page for answer

"So I made a list of ten items that I thought might work… #1 was to go meet the owner of the property across the street and see if there was a compromise we could work out."

269

270

"Me too, Beth, and it occurred twenty years ago.
At the time my wife and I had four young children.
We had a nice home with a big mortgage and two
expensive cars. I was really frightened as I had no
net below me.

"But I keep plugging … made a list of ten more
items that might work. NADA… NADA … NADA."

"I was very scared, Beth! I feared that Calvin Coolidge's
words were dated. But I knew I had to persist.

"I decided to double check all my assumptions. In
Connecticut a property owner within 100 feet of a rezoned
property has an absolute right to challenge in court a
rezoning. So I decided to recheck the distance between
my property and that of the owner across the street."

"And you know what, Beth. With help from a surveyor I discovered that an earlier measurement had been done incorrectly, and that the distance between my property and the one across the street was actually 100 **and FIVE feet!** In other words, I had the right to go to court and contest the validity of the lawsuit!"

273

274

275

276

"And you can too, Beth. The truth about achievement is almost always a story of persistence and tenacity. Those who stay the course, no matter what the setbacks, usually prevail and reach their goals. Those who don't are the ones who miss life's opportunities."

"I have a lot to think about, Jim…Thanks for your time."

I have thought a lot about persistence, and I have identified four reasons why I believe it is most often the critical ingredient to success.

1. The longer you work at something, the more perspective you bring to it.

Have you ever done a crossword or jigsaw puzzle and put it aside – stuck? Then you come back a few hours later and all of a sudden you see things that you did not see before. That is because every minute of the day you are operating under certain stimuli; when those conditions change, so do your insights and perspectives.

"That inspiration comes, does not depend on me. The only thing I can do is make sure it catches me working."

Pablo Picasso

2. The longer you work at something, the better you get at it.

It is, as you know, the premise of this book that "talent" – the graceful and elegant performance of a particular skill – is the result of many hours of practice and repetition.

Persistence works because the more you work at something, the better you get at it, and with excellence comes success.

"That which we persist in doing becomes easier – not that the nature of the task has changed, but our ability to do it has increased."

Ralph Waldo Emerson

3. The longer you work at something, the greater the likelihood that you will be in action when your "ship comes in."

I operate under the assumption that most of us get a certain number of good opportunities in life. As long as you are persisting in the pursuit of your goal, you will be "in play" when a unique opportunity arises.

"All of us have bad luck and good luck. The man who persists through the bad luck – who keeps going – is the man who is there when the good luck comes – and is ready to receive it."

Robert Collier, author and publisher

4. The longer you work at something, the greater the probability that you will wear down the opposition.

When you persevere, whoever or whatever is standing in the way of your success will often tire before you do. When you persist, you erode the will of the forces in your path.

"To audition at places like Catch a Rising Star and The Improv, we would start lining up outside the clubs at two in the afternoon with hopes of getting onstage sometime after eleven that night. You'd spend the whole day sitting on the curb, waiting and waiting. Inevitably, somebody in front of you would say, 'This stinks!' and walk away. I always enjoyed that. All of a sudden, I had moved up ... my standing in show business had just improved!"

Leading with My Chin, Jay Leno

Just for fun, I thought I would give you a few snippets of famous people who had to persevere against the opinions of those standing in the way of their success:

Elvis – tried out at the Grand Ole Opry in Nashville and was told that he should keep driving a truck.

Marilyn Monroe – a producer told her she did not have the right look for the movies.

Dr. Seuss – turned down by the first 28 publishers who saw his manuscripts. Went on to be one of the most successful authors ever.

Michael Jordan – could not make his high school basketball team.

283

THERE ARE THOUSANDS AND THOUSANDS OF STORIES OF LESS FAMOUS PEOPLE WHO WERE NOT DISCOURAGED BY REJECTION.

THE REASON "EXPERTS" ARE OFTEN WRONG IS THAT SUCCESS IS NOT JUST ABOUT WHAT IS VISIBLE. THE TRUE KEYS TO SUCCESS – HEART AND WILL – CANNOT BE SEEN AT FIRST GLANCE.

284

Speaking of persistence, I have to persist in trying to convince Billy that the path to success as a comedian is longer and harder than he believes. And, flipping the coin over, I have to convince Beth that her fears of public speaking can be addressed over time, and that her desire to be in politics should not end just because of one painful defeat.

285

So, I invited Billy and Beth to my home.

286

287

288

"I understand, Beth. And you could lose the next election you enter. But, I have learned something important about persistence I want to share with you. The more you persist, the better you get at it."

"Jim, that feels like a *non sequitur* to me."

289

YOU ARE ABOUT TO LEARN ONE OF THE GREAT TRUTHS ABOUT PERSISTENCE:

THE MORE YOU STICK THINGS OUT, THE BETTER YOU GET AT STICKING THINGS OUT...

290

"Not really, Beth, let me explain. In thinking about how I was able to persist when I was in trouble with that deal in Shelton, I concluded that prior challenges had prepared me. I had been in corners before and had learned that I could fight my way out of trouble."

"I am starting to understand what you are saying, and it made me think of something."

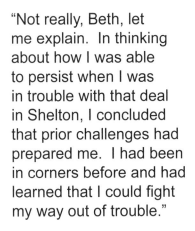

"I have run in several marathons. In my first marathon I was doing OK and then all of a sudden at the 20th mile, I hit the proverbial wall. I felt like I just could not go on and I considered quitting. But I did not, and by the 22nd mile I was feeling better and I finished the race.

When I ran my second marathon a few months later, I once again experienced a rush of fatigue and fear at the 20-mile mark. Again I wondered if I could finish. **But, this time I had something to fall back on: I recalled exactly how I felt at the 20th mile in my first marathon.** I recalled the panic I felt. And I recalled that by just putting one foot in front of the other, I was able finish the race.

In other words, by persisting the first time, I was better able to persist the second time!"

"Beth, that's a great example of the point I want to make. Both the desire to quit and the will to persevere are states of mind. By pushing yourself through one adversity, you build your ability to push past future challenges."

293

Some people believe that the ability to persist has to do with one's upbringing or some kind of genetic predisposition. Perhaps you can hear me thinking "talent, schmalent?" That is because, as with other attributes critical to success, I believe a person can develop mechanisms which build their strength to deal with adversity.

What follows are my suggestions:

294

STRENGTHEN YOUR ABILITY TO DEAL WITH CHALLENGE

1. Challenge yourself in increments. As you would build your endurance for an athletic event (such as a marathon), you can build your fortitude with smaller challenges. Each time you test yourself and persist, you increase your ability to take on a bigger test.

2. Optimize your energy level. Persistence is ultimately about energy. As General Douglas McArthur said, "fatigue makes cowards of us all." A healthy lifestyle maintains and builds energy, positioning you as well as possible to beat back setback.

3. Remind yourself of your goals every daily. I have a picture of an island in the Caribbean that I would like to buy someday. I look at it every day. It builds my resolve. I look at it two or three times a day when I am feeling down and tired.

4. Learn and practice techniques for mind control. As we have discussed, mental fortitude is a skill that can be acquired. I am always looking for suggestions in this regard. I recently reread one of Tony Robbins books on neuro-linguistic programming (NLP).

5. Disconnect from critical self-judgment. Some people quit too soon because they get down on themselves. Learn to like yourself. Admire yourself for taking on a challenge that others might shirk. Climbing a mountain means slipping at times. Everyone slips.

"Jim, you are actually starting to make sense. Still, I think I can find a way to get on *The Tonight Show*. I am clever. I can make people laugh. I am good looking.

296

"You are good looking, Billy. And perhaps you will find a short cut to *The Tonight Show*. I hope you do."

OY YOI YOI...

"Thanks, Jim... I think you are good looking, too."

297

THREE YEARS LATER

Billy tried stand-up. It was harder than he had anticipated. He concluded that the path to making a living in comedy was too long and arduous for him. So, he did some self-analysis and decided that his desire to entertain people could be expressed in other ways.

BILLY GOT A JOB TEACHING ACCOUNTING AT A COMMUNITY COLLEGE.

300

AND HE BROUGHT HUMOR INTO HIS CLASSROOM.

"Hey, I did that on purpose."

301

As for Beth, well she worked at her public speaking …
and worked at it and worked at it. And she actually got
pretty good at it. So she decided to run for her town's
zoning commission, and she was elected! What's more,
she was so well respected by the other members of the
commission, she was elected chairwoman.

"As chairwoman of the Town of
Springfield Planning and Zoning
Commission, I hereby call this
meeting to order."

I am proud of Billy and Beth. They identified what was really important to them … what their passions were. They then threw all their energies into their chosen endeavor. Each persisted against setbacks and today both are where they would like to be (although Beth has her eye on a State senate seat).

304

THE
END

305

I hope you've enjoyed Billy and Beth's story.

They asked me to make a list of what I consider to be the ten most important characteristics of highly successful people. Their hope is that you will use that information to help in your own quest for achievement.

MY TOP TEN LIST

1. Success stories commonly boil down to tales of ordinary people who had the courage to take action in the pursuit of something they felt strongly about, and the will to persist against all setbacks.

In many situations the difference between those who succeed and those who do not is about the width of an egg shell. In other words, there is not much distinction between the person who makes it big, and the person who does not.

Usually the difference is about guts – the willingness to act in the pursuit of one's passion and the courage to stay the course no matter what the strength of the headwinds.

Too many people believe that success is reserved for the special individual. That is not the case. Do you remember the scene in *The Wizard of Oz* when Dorothy's dog, Toto, pulled back the curtain hiding the wizard? And what we saw was a very ordinary little man working hard at lots of levers and dials. That is the story of many successful individuals. When you pull back the curtain on the story of their lives, they are just ordinary folks who worked very hard at pursuing their aspirations.

2. Successful people prepare for the journey from where they are to where they want to be.

Billy was not prepared for the length and difficulty of passage that was required to make a living as a stand-up comic.

By preparing your mind for what lies ahead, you are better able to deal with adversity. When the inevitable crosswinds come, your mind **defaults to**:

"Ah yes, I have been expecting problems – I did not know exactly what they would be but I knew they would come sooner or later."

As opposed to:

"Oh no!! This can't be happening!! Why is everything so much harder for me than for everybody else? Why can't I catch a break. OH NO!"

I am exaggerating a bit of but the point is very important. Paraphrasing Dr. Scott Peck (*The Road Less Traveled*):

Achieving the success you want will be difficult. But, once you know that it will be difficult, the journey is no longer quite as difficult. Once you know that your journey will be fraught with challenge, you are better able to deal with the adversities that come upon you.

3. Successful people do everything they can to maximize the probability of their success.

There are no guarantees in life. So, successful people do whatever they can to stack the odds in their favor. Here are some examples.

1. Successful people take nothing for granted. They know that the "devil is in the details" and so they leave no stone unturned in their pursuit of success.

2. Successful people believe in constant improvement. The Japanese have a word, "kaizen," which means daily improvement. I find most successful folks to be curious, to be readers, and to be good listeners.

3. Successful people pick their spots. No one can be good at everything. Many big achievers identify what they are good at, and then do whatever they can to become really expert. They recognize the validity of the saying "Jack of all trades, master of none."

4. Successful people network. Successful people understand that 95% of the time, one's success is dependent upon other people. If those who hold the keys to your kingdom know and like you, you are much more likely to cross the finish line.

5. Successful people treat all people with respect. Most success stories I know operate under the principle that "one should be gracious to everyone on the way up because you never know who you might meet on the way down."

6. Successful people don't wait for good things to happen. Once they identify what stands between them and their goals, they pull a Nike and "just do it."

"Successful people ... become successful by establishing the habit of doing things unsuccessful people don't like to do. Successful people don't always like to do these things either ... they just do them nevertheless."

The Common Denominator of Success, E. N. Gray

4. Successful people take action.

At some point successful people stop deliberating and take action. They realize that they cannot control every possible eventuality that may result. Their attitude is that they can deal with whatever happens. So, they do not let opportunities pass them by while they dally to analyze lots of plusses and minuses.

Taking action can be a confidence builder. Once you start acting, you begin to see your own competence at work. Alternatively, those who don't take action, never give themselves a chance to discover what they can do as and when they need to. As a result, inaction feeds upon itself.

"When people shun an activity out of doubt over personal competence, they participate in the self-destructive process of retarding their own development. Further, the more they avoid such activities, the more entrenched self-doubt becomes because doubters never get the chance to prove themselves wrong."

Understanding Motivation and Emotion
Professor John Reeve, University of Iowa

"Success ... action. Successful people keep moving."

**Conrad Hilton,
Founder of Hilton Hotels**

5. Successful people learn to combat the fear of failure.

Everyone fears failure. Successful people sublimate fear when they need to move forward.

An event(s) of failure is part of the life of almost every successful person. But, that event does not prevent another try. The fear cannot become crippling.

"Even the worst of failures is not what it seems. One surprising piece of advice sometimes given by highly successful people is this: 'Fail soon, fail often.' This does sound odd, but the explanation is simple. Anyone not experiencing failure is not launching out into new territory."

True Success
Tom Morris

Like the first time you rode a two-wheeled bicycle, once you start moving as fast as you can, the world takes on a whole new perspective. Any action involves the prospect of failure (as does that first spin on a two-wheeler), but by avoiding any ride that might involve failure, you are missing a lot of life's journey.

"It's incredibly important to understand that failing is part of learning. ... By avoiding failure, you're also avoiding life's richness. And what happens if you fail? It can be liberating."

Maria Shriver
Commencement Address,
May, 1998

6. Successful people work on their mental fortitude.

Mental strength is not something you are born with. It is something you can develop, something you can build.

You can learn to control the thoughts in your mind. You can learn to support the positive and reject the negative. You can learn to insert powerful dominating thoughts in the stead of destructive ones.

An ability to choose the thoughts you want, those thoughts that will take you forward in the direction you want to go, is a critical component of success.

"Human beings can alter their lives by altering their attitudes of mind."

The Principles of Psychology
William James

"You can choose how you think about your problems and other opponents all the time. Your power of choice is your greatest power...Some see an opponent and notice only the threatening aspect. Others see the very same opponent and are able to respond to the chance it offers for victory."

A writing from *The Code of the Samurai Warrior*

The Samurai ruled Japan for 700 years.

7. Successful people train themselves to see the glass half-full.

Success and optimism are interrelated. Those who see a glass half-full tend to create a self-fulfilling prophecy: by approaching their endeavor as if good things are going to happen, oftentimes good things **do happen**.

In 1934 a woman named Dorothea Brande wrote a book titled, *Wake Up and Live*. This book became an instant best seller with one simple message: **success is inevitable** when one acts as if it is impossible to fail. Ms. Brande studied people for many years and concluded that those who were able to instill in their mind the conviction that failure was not a possibility **always found a way to succeed**.

"You will find that if you can imaginatively capture the state of mind which would be yours if you knew you were going towards a prearranged and inevitable success, the first result will be a tremendous surge of vitality, of freshness."

Wake Up and Live

There are many stories of people who achieved great success in spite of all the naysayers simply because the successful person took action with a positive, optimistic attitude.

"Maybe I've just had too many experiences in my life where what I've accomplished was never supposed to happen to me. I was never even supposed to have a film career."

Michael Moore, filmmaker and Academy Award winner
explaining his optimism

8. Successful people are very hard workers.

"There are no secrets to success. It is the result of preparation, hard work, and learning from failure."

General Colin Powell (ret.)

Success does not ensue from a "pretty good" effort. You want success? Think 1,000% effort. There is no substitute for hard work.

The good news is that with hard work, we can optimize our innate aptitudes and enhance the probability of our success. But first comes the hard work: throwing everything you have into the attainment of your dream, leaving nothing on the table.

One of my favorite quotes comes from the great showman and entrepreneur, P.T. Barnum:

"Whatever you do, do with all your might. Work at it if necessary early and late, in season and out of season, not leaving a stone unturned, and never deferring for a single hour that which you can be doing just as well now. ... Many a man acquires a fortune by doing his business thoroughly, while his neighbor remains poor for life because he only half does his business."

9. Successful people persevere.

There is nothing more important than persistence. Whatever you undertake, you are going to experience setbacks. What you do when those setbacks arise will determine your future.

Successful people never give up on something important to them. It may take years for them to get from Point A to Point B, but they never stop trying. There is just no accounting for what you can do once you set your mind.

One of my personal heroes is Teddy Roosevelt, the 26th President of the United States.

Teddy Roosevelt was born asthmatic and sickly. He looked so ill on birth that his mother described him as a "terrapin." Teddy's first few years were very difficult as he suffered from many illnesses and ailments.

When Teddy was 12 years old, his father had a conversation with the frail boy:

"Theodore," the big man said to his son, *"you have the mind but not the body, and without the help of the body, the mind cannot go as far as it should. You must make your body."*

It is reported that young Teddy jerked his head back and replied to his father through clenched teeth:

"I'll make my body!"

From that day on, young Teddy put himself through an incredibly demanding physical regimen and with unwavering tenacity, converted his physique from sickly to robust. The successful people I know have "Teddy Roosevelt tenacity."

10. Successful people believe in right and wrong.

I am not going to tell you that every successful person is a wonderfully decent man or woman … and nor that every honorable person achieves the success he or she aspires to.

I do, however, believe that decency in one's heart increases the likelihood of his or her success. I cannot give you a scientific explanation although I believe that the integrity-success connection is about energy.

"Integrity creates a force field of aliveness, energy, and creativity … Integrity works. It is not just a noble idea. It is a crucial set of operating principles."

The Corporate Mystic, Hendricks and Ludeman

Finally, here is advice from a Commencement Address Oprah Winfrey gave in June 2008 to the graduating class at Stanford University:

"It's a lesson that applies to all our lives … What matters most is what's inside. What matters most is the sense of integrity, of quality and beauty."

Note: all three of our research team's favorite commencement speeches are referenced in this book – given by Jodie Foster, Maria Shriver and Oprah Winfrey.

*"If I were two-faced, would
I be wearing this one?"*

Abraham Lincoln

"It's not the critic who counts, nor the man who points out how the strong man stumbled, or where the doer of deeds could have done better. The credit belongs to the man who is actually in the arena, whose face is marred by dust and sweat and blood, who strives valiantly, who errs and comes short again and again, who knows the great enthusiasm, the great devotion, and spends himself in a worthy cause, who at best knows achievement and who at worst if he fails at least fails while daring greatly so that his place shall never be with those cold and timid souls who know neither victory nor defeat."

Teddy Roosevelt

POSTSCRIPT

One of the hot, new shows on TV right now is *Glee*, starring Lea Michele.

"This is all I have ever wanted to do since I was 8 years old!"

CONCLUSION

Well that concludes our skinny book. We hope you have enjoyed it.

For further readings on the subjects we covered, please see the Bibliography.

As always, I would love to hear from you.

My e-mail is jrandel@theskinnyon.com

With warm regards,

Jim Randel

FURTHER READING

Here is a list of some of the books we reviewed in preparing *The Skinny on Success:*

Action, Robert Ringer (Evan, 2004)

Amazing Stories of Survival (Time, Inc. 2006)

Awaken the Giant Within, Anthony Robbins (Pocket Books, 1991)

Beyond Positive Thinking, Robert Anthony (Morgan James, 2007)

Born Standing Up, Steve Martin (Scribner, 2007)

Chicken Soup for the Soul, Canfield and Hansen (Heath, 2001)

Dare to Dream, John Maxwell (Thomas Nelson, 2006)

Defying Gravity, Prill Boyle (Emmis, 2004)

Dreams from My Father, Barack Obama (Three Rivers Press, 1995)

Do What You Love, The Money Will Follow, Marsha Sinetar (Dell, 1987)

Do You!, Russell Simmons (Gotham, 2007)

Famous Failures, Joey Green (Lunatic Press, 2007)

Finding Your Own North Star, Martha Beck (Three Rivers Press, 2001)

Flow, Mihaly Csikszentmihalyi (Harper & Row, 1992)

Game of My Life, Ken Palmer (Sports Publishing, 2007)

Get in the Game, Cal Ripkin (Gotham, 2008)

Great Failures of the Extremely Successful, Steve Young (Tallfellow, 2002)

Henry Thoreau, Robert Richardson, Jr. (University of California Press, 1986)

Houdini, Kenneth Silverman (HarperCollins, 1996)

How to Win Friends and Influence People, Dale Carnegie (Pocket Books, 1936)

How Successful People Think, John Maxwell (Center Street, 2009)

I'm Chevy Chase ... And You're Not, Rena Fruchter (Virgin Books, 2007)

It's Not About the Bike, Lance Armstrong (Putnam, 2000)

John Glenn, A Memoir, John Glenn (Bantam, 1999)

Jump In!, Mark Burnett (Ballantine, 2005)

Just Do It, Donald Katz (Adams Media, 1994)

Late Bloomers, Brendan Gill (Artisan, 1996)

Leading with My Chin, Jay Leno (Harper, 1996)

Leonardo DaVinci, Sherwin Nuland (Penguin, 2000)

Life Entrepreneurs, Gergen and Vanourek (Wiley, 2008)

Lone Survivor, Marcus Lattrell (Little Brown, 2007)

Losing My Virginity, Richard Branson (Three Rivers Press, 1998)

Lucky Man, Michael J. Fox (Hyperion, 2002)

Make It Happen, Kevin Liles (Atria, 2005)

Mindset: The New Psychology of Success, Carol Dweck (Ballantine, 2006)

Never Give Up, Donald Trump (Wiley, 2008)

No Such Thing as a Bad Day, Hamilton Jordan (Longstreet Press, 2000)

Now, Discover Your Strengths (Buckingham and Clifton (Simon & Schuster, 2001)

Oprah Winfrey, Katherine Krohn (A&E, 2002)

Outliers, Malcolm Gladwell (Little Brown, 2008)

Positivity, Barbara Fredrickson (Crown, 2009)

Rocket Boys, Homer Hickham (Delta, 1998)

Secrets of Becoming a Late Bloomer, Goldman and Mahler (Stillpoint, 1995)

Stick To It, C. Leslie Charles (Yes, 1995)

Success, Jena Pinchot (Random House, 2005)

Success Through a Positive Mental Attitude, Hill and Stone (Pocket Books, 1960)

Swimming Across, Andrew Grove (Warner Books, 2001)

Talent, Tom Peters (DK Publishing, 2005)

Talent is Never Enough, John Maxwell (Thomas Nelson, 2007)

Talent is Overrated, Geoff Colvin (Penguin, 2008)

Ten Things I Wish I'd Known – Before I Went Out Into The Real World, Maria Shriver (Warner Books, 2000)

The Element, Ken Robinson (Viking, 2009)

The Life of P.T. Barnum, Barnum (1855)

The Life You Imagine, Derek Jeter (Three Rivers Press, 2000)

The Magic of Thinking Big, David Schwartz (Fireside, 1959)

The Power of Focus, Canfield, Hansen, Hewitt (Heath Communications, 2000)

The Power of Now, Eckhart Tolle (Namaste, 1999)

The Road Less Traveled, M. Scott Peck (Touchstone, 1978)

The Rise of Theodore Roosevelt, Edmund Morris (Coward, McCann, 1979)

The Talent Code, Daniel Coyne (Bantam, 2009)

The Truth About Winning, Tom Veneziano (Veneziano Enterprises, 2001)

The Winning Spirit, Joe Montana (Ballantine, 2005)

The X Factor, George Plimpton (Whittle, 1990)

True North, Bill George (Wiley, 2007)

Unstoppable, Cynthia Kersey (Sourcebooks, 1998)

Wake Up and Live, Dorothea Brande (1936)

What Makes the Great Great, Dennis Kimbro (Doubleday, 1995)

When Pride Still Mattered, David Maraniss (Touchstone, 1999)

*Answer to question in panel 266:
Calvin Coolidge is pictured in the middle photo on the bottom row.

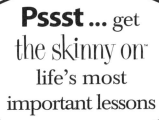